Facts About the Ball Python

By Lisa Strattin

© 2019 Lisa Strattin

Revised 2022 © Lisa Strattin

FREE BOOK

FREE FOR ALL SUBSCRIBERS

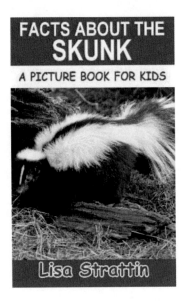

LisaStrattin.com/Subscribe-Here

BOX SET

- **FACTS ABOUT THE POISON DART FROGS**
- **FACTS ABOUT THE THREE TOED SLOTH**
  - **FACTS ABOUT THE RED PANDA**
  - **FACTS ABOUT THE SEAHORSE**
  - **FACTS ABOUT THE PLATYPUS**
  - **FACTS ABOUT THE REINDEER**
  - **FACTS ABOUT THE PANTHER**
- **FACTS ABOUT THE SIBERIAN HUSKY**

LisaStrattin.com/BookBundle

Facts for Kids Picture Books by Lisa Strattin

Little Blue Penguin, Vol 92

Chipmunk, Vol 5

Frilled Lizard, Vol 39

Blue and Gold Macaw, Vol 13

Poison Dart Frogs, Vol 50

Blue Tarantula, Vol 115

African Elephants, Vol 8

Amur Leopard, Vol 89

Sabre Tooth Tiger, Vol 167

Baboon, Vol 174

Sign Up for New Release Emails Here

LisaStrattin.com/subscribe-here

★★COVER IMAGE★★

https://www.flickr.com/photos/reptilarium/6923762999/

★★ADDITIONAL IMAGES★★

https://www.flickr.com/photos/robertnelson/16624577548/

https://www.flickr.com/photos/robertnelson/16624577878/

https://www.flickr.com/photos/scubabrett22/17053442659/

https://www.flickr.com/photos/32152408@N05/3012950792/

https://www.flickr.com/photos/lesliesciencenaturecenter/6211872520/

https://www.flickr.com/photos/mariposavet/15659401730/

https://www.flickr.com/photos/briangratwicke/5110315523/

https://www.flickr.com/photos/8373783@N07/3050676193/

https://www.flickr.com/photos/132295270@N07/28809385538/

https://www.flickr.com/photos/nickseeger/3050680736/

Contents

INTRODUCTION

The Ball Python is a medium-sized snake found in central and western Africa. It is called the Ball Python because it has a tendency to curl up in a ball if it is startled or scared. It is also known as the royal python because the African royalty liked to keep them as pets and even to wear them as though they were a necklace

Ball Pythons can be found in hot and dry regions in Benin, Cameroon, Central African Republic, Chad, Ghana, Guinea, Guinea-Bissau, Ivory Coast, Liberia, Mali, Nigeria, Senegal, Sierra Leone, Sudan, and Uganda. In many places they are hunted as food and used for leather products. In others they are revered as a symbol of the earth and are well cared for. Some cultures will even perform funeral services when a Ball Python is killed.

CHARACTERISTICS

Ball Pythons are timid snakes. They are terrestrial, meaning that they are found on the ground rather than in trees. This allows them to live in habitats close to human habitation where there are lots of mice and rats to eat. Ball Pythons are very useful for pest control. This may also be why wild Ball Pythons are commonly exposed to parasites.

Ball Pythons have become very popular in the pet snake world. They are smaller and more docile than many of the other python species, and they can be bred in a variety of colors. One downside is that they commonly hide in an enclosure, by a rock, or in a tree stump in their cage or pet enclosure. In nature they would hide in an abandoned termite mound or animal burrow.

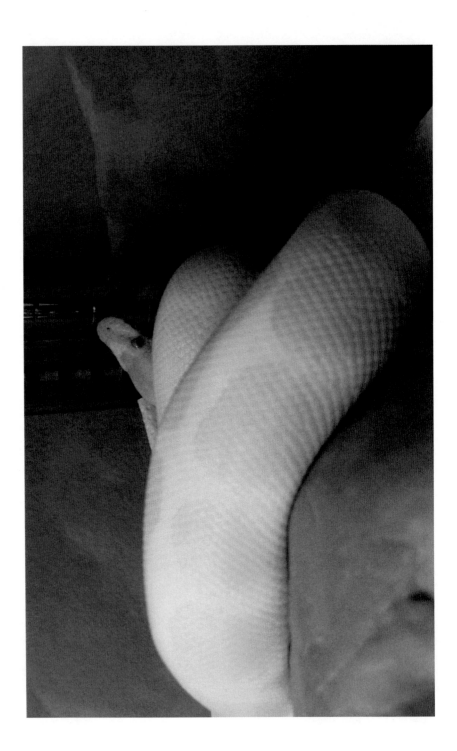

APPEARANCE

Ball Pythons are long and stocky. They have a small head with a long forked tongue and no visible ears. The body is black or brown with pale blotches along the back and sides, although they can be bred to show many colors. Ball Pythons are covered with smooth scales, and they shed their skin from time to time.

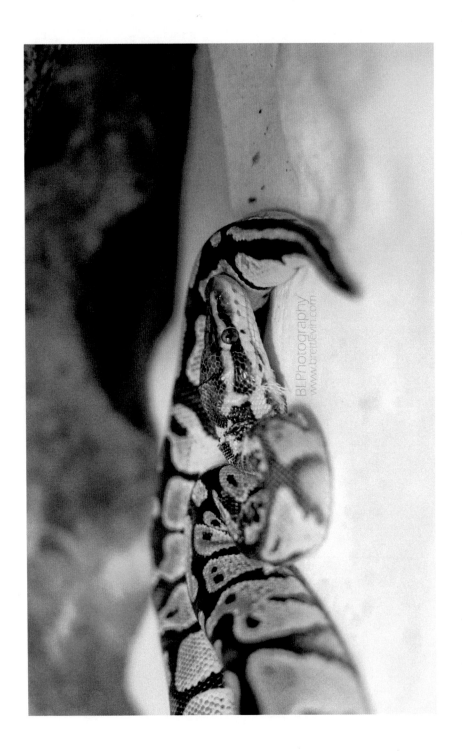

LIFE STAGES

Ball Pythons have two main life stages: juveniles and adults. The female will lay between 3 and 11 eggs in a nest, and she will incubate them to keep them warm until they are ready to hatch. This will take about two months. After this point they will hatch into juveniles. When they are this young they are also called hatchlings. They will mature into adults in about 12 to 18 months.

LIFE SPAN

Ball Pythons live a lot longer in captivity than they do in the wild. This is likely due to better food availability and better care by pet owners. In the wild they are faced with parasites and diseases. A wild Ball Python is expected to live for 10 or 15 years, while a captive Ball Python will likely live for 20 to 30 years. The oldest recorded Ball Python lived to be 47 years old, as of this writing.

SIZE

Ball Pythons can grow up to five or six feet long, which is considerably shorter than most other types of pythons. They can weigh from eight to ten pounds as fully grown adults. As with many snake species, females tend to be larger than males. One recorded Ball Python was said to be over seven feet long and weighed as much as 15 pounds!

HABITAT

Ball Pythons live in western and central Africa where it is very hot. They live mostly in grass and tree savannah where there are few trees, but it is not too dense. They often live in old termite mounds and other holes left by animals like badgers or rabbits.

They thrive in hot and dry areas and can be found on agricultural land. They are great at catching mice and rats and help keep the rodent population down.

DIET

Ball Pythons are carnivores that catch their prey and constrict them using their strong muscles until they suffocate. They primarily feed on small mammals such as rats, mice, and shrews, but will also take small birds. They do not need to eat every day and may take several days to digest a meal. They will also sometimes stop eating in the winter when it gets very cold.

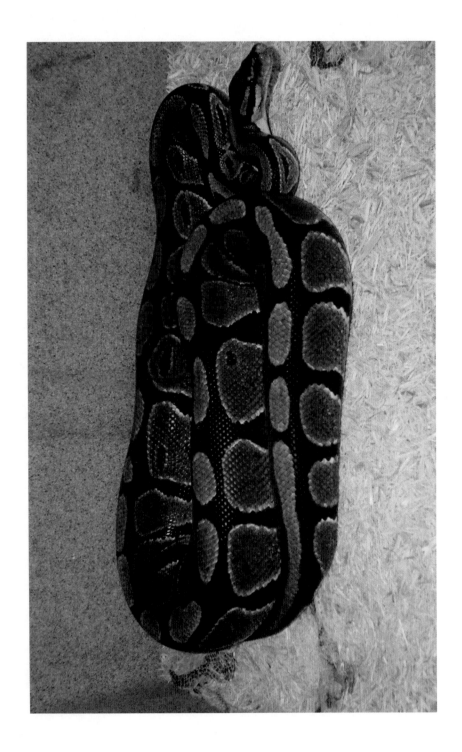

FRIENDS AND ENEMIES

Ball Pythons are predators and so do not have many friends in the wild. Their main friend is considered to be human companions, particularly the Igpo people in southern Nigeria, who see the python as special and treat it with great respect.

It is also a very popular snake in the pet trade which means that people will take young pythons from the wild. There is currently no legislation protecting this species.

Small rodents and birds consider the Ball Python to be an enemy as it will often catch them as prey.

SUITABILITY AS PETS

Ball Pythons are commonly kept as pets as they do not grow as large as some of the other pythons, and they have a gentle personality. Even though they are a docile species, care needs to be taken around them as they are constrictors and could accidentally hurt a child or another pet.

COLOR ME

COLOR ME

COLOR ME

COLOR ME

COLOR ME

COLOR ME

COLOR ME

COLOR ME

COLOR ME

COLOR ME

Please leave me a review here:

LisaStrattin.com/Review-Vol-176

For more Kindle Downloads Visit Lisa Strattin Author Page on Amazon Author Central

amazon.com/author/lisastrattin

To see upcoming titles, visit my website at LisaStrattin.com– most books available on Kindle!

LisaStrattin.com

FREE BOOK

FOR ALL SUBSCRIBERS – SIGN UP NOW

LisaStrattin.com/Subscribe-Here

LisaStrattin.com/Facebook

LisaStrattin.com/Youtube

Made in the USA
Coppell, TX
11 December 2023

25897961R00026